ARTS & CRAFTS

JAMES MASSEY & SHIRLEY MAXWELL

ABBEVILLE
STYLEBOOKS™

ABBEVILLE PRESS · PUBLISHERS

NEW YORK · LONDON · PARIS

CONTENTS

Introduction 6

THE PROGRESSIVE ERA 9
With reform in the air, opportunities opened up for workers and women, children and capitalists.

ART IN CRAFT 18
Handcraftsmanship became the ideal, and proponents dedicated themselves to simplicity, utility, and unity.

OUTSIDE 28
Arts and Crafts buildings took on varied dress, but honest materials, honestly treated, became the norm.

INSIDE 38
Interiors were warm and natural, enriched with built-in fixtures and—at the center of family life—the hearth.

FINISHING TOUCHES 49
Craft was king, from pottery to metalwork, and all could be appreciated from a relaxing Morris chair.

IN STYLE 70
At home, at work, at play, at large, and on the road, Arts and Crafts structures exemplified human scale and the comforts of a cozy retreat from the machine age.

Sources of Information 90

Additional Sites to Visit 91

Recommended Reading 92

Index 93   Credits 95

INTRODUCTION

"Have nothing in your houses that you do not know to be useful, or believe to be beautiful."
—William Morris, "Hopes and Fears for Art," 1882

L ondon's Great Exhibition of 1851, the first of many international shows that would celebrate the wares of industrializing countries in the nineteenth century, brought divergent reactions from those who saw it at the fabulous Crystal Palace. Some were thrilled by the number, variety, and technological virtuosity of the machine-made objects showcased in the exhibition. Others were appalled by the poor design of those same objects, which they regarded as poisonous fruit of the industrial process.

Revulsion toward machines and their products—including the dehumanization of work and the degradation of the worker—seethed during the remainder of the century and well into the next. It was strongest in England, where the industrial revolution had begun and where industrialism had wreaked its most obvious horrors.

This protest against modern industrialism emerged from the mid-nineteenth-century Gothic Revival movement, which urged a return to medieval standards of morality and craftsmanship. Building on the ideas of the English critic John Ruskin, later reformers demanded buildings and objects that were useful, beautiful, honest in their treatment of materials, well made, and affordable. Whether they could—or should—also be achievable by machine processes would become a point of much disagreement.

By the end of the nineteenth century, reform efforts had shifted from reviving the Gothic church style to advocating a simplified and unified total environment in which art and industry, artist and artisan, design and social reform would be inextricably linked. In 1888 the Arts and Crafts Exhibition Society, composed of several influential English theorists, architects, and artists, issued a call for a major national exhibition to illustrate these goals. The exhibit announcement was the first official use of the term "Arts and Crafts." With its name established, the movement was propelled along the path it would follow until World War I drowned out its arguments.

William Morris—English designer, social critic, poet, and author—stepped from his prominent role in the Gothic Revival to found the multinational adventure that became the Arts and Crafts movement. Leading by exhortation and example, Morris and his colleagues, such as Ruskin and the American Gustav Stickley, embarked on a quest for simplicity and unity of design in architecture, landscape architecture, and the decorative arts; recognition of the individual artist and craftsman; rehumanization of work; and excellent design for all.

Because English proponents vehemently opposed the use of machines, their goal of beautiful objects and homes for every class was doomed. Only the rich could afford such skilled handwork. Americans, however, viewed the machine as the artist's assistant, and the United States embraced a mass-produced Arts and Crafts aesthetic.

The years between the end of the American Civil War (1865) and World War I (1914) were a tumultuous time in which many people found, at best, an uneasy peace with the machine ethic. The Arts and Crafts movement formed a sturdy bridge that carried precepts of morality and beauty from their Victorian infancy into the modern age. These ideals were shaped and reshaped to fit the changing needs of the individual and modern society.

A near-utopian scheme, Rock Crest–Rock Glen was conceived in 1912 for Mason City, Iowa, by Walter Burley Griffin and drawn by Marion Mahony Griffin.

DANCING TO A NEW BEAT

Genius is one per cent inspiration and ninety-nine per cent perspiration.
—Thomas Edison,
Life, 1932

Anticipating the moving picture, Eadweard Muybridge (1830–1904) used sequential still cameras to produce the animated images published in his 1887 book, *Animal Locomotion*.

Technological change burst like a meteor shower on the final years of Queen Victoria's long reign. Telephones, electric lights, indoor plumbing, phonographs, radios, express trains, and automobiles—Victoria's world was forever transformed. New materials from reinforced concrete to rayon opened unguessed-of avenues.

Conflict between nations and social classes was endemic. England faced the Crimean and Boer Wars and the Zulu Uprising while gaining or consolidating far-flung territory. Europe engaged in endless partitions and reconstitutions of states (Prussia, Italy, Austro-Hungary, Greece, Turkey, Armenia) as well as colonization abroad. The plight of

the worker stirred strong interest in social reform and the tenets of socialism.

A string of mostly one-term presidents in America led to the period of dazzling social change known as the Progressive Era, presided over by Theodore Roosevelt and Woodrow Wilson. The Spanish-American War provided U.S. footholds in the Philippines and Puerto Rico. Western territories tumbled into statehood, bringing the total number of stars on the American banner to forty-eight by 1912. The flag was planted at both poles. Magazines and musical comedies enlightened and enlivened public taste, and the period that had entered on a Strauss waltz went out to the strains of ragtime and jazz.

The descendants of Thomas Edison's 1877 "talking machine" brought home the sound of music. This improved "flower horn" was new in 1908.

1886 1887 1888 1889 1890 1891 1892 1893 1894 1895 1896 1897 1898 1899 1900 1901

POLITICS & SOCIETY

■ American Federation of Labor founded

■ G.E. makes electric motors

■ Kodak perfects box camera

■ Six London women murdered by "Jack the Ripper"

■ Hull House opens in Chicago

Basketball originated ■
in Springfield, Mass.

U.S. annexes Hawaii ■

Dreyfus convicted of treason ■

■ Cuba wages war of independence from Spain

■ Marconi invents radio telegraphy

■ Motion picture camera invented

■ First modern Olympics held in Athens

Spanish-American War fought ■

Walter Reed finds cause of yellow fever ■

McKinley assassinated; Theodore ■
Roosevelt becomes U.S. president

Edward VII succeeds Queen Victoria ■

LITERATURE & PERFORMING ARTS

■ Dr. Jekyll and Mr. Hyde (Stevenson)

■ Little Lord Fauntleroy (Burnett)

■ The Yeoman of the Guard (Gilbert and Sullivan)

The Nutcracker (Tchaikovsky) ■

"New World" Symphony (Dvořák) ■

Swan Lake (Tchaikovsky) ■

The Time Machine ■
(Wells)

La Bohème ■
(Puccini)

■ The Picture of Dorian Gray (Wilde)

Finlandia (Sibelius) ■

L'Après-midi d'un Faune (Debussy) ■

■ "The Stars and Stripes Forever" (Sousa)

■ Captains Courageous (Kipling)

■ Cyrano de Bergerac (Rostand)

■ The Turn of the Screw (James)

Cakewalk dance popularity ■

Claudine à l'école ■
(Colette)

Lord Jim (Conrad) ■

VISUAL ARTS & DESIGN

■ The Kiss (Rodin)

■ Last Impressionist exhibition, Paris

■ Arts and Crafts Exhibition Society

■ Eiffel Tower (Eiffel)

■ Home and Studio (Wright)

Foster House (Voysey) ■

Morris's Kelmscott Press ■

At the Moulin Rouge ■
(Toulouse-Lautrec)

Hubbard's Roycroft Community ■

■ Standen (Webb)

■ Munstead Wood Garden (Jekyll)

Garden city concept ■
(Howard)

Austellungshaus der Wiener Sezession (Olbrich)

Stickley's Craftsman Workshops ■

The Orchard (Voysey) ■

The Craftsman ■

1886 1887 1888 1889 1890 1891 1892 1893 1894 1895 1896 1897 1898 1899 1900 1901

1902 1903 1904 1905 1906 1907 1908 1909 1910 1911 1912 1913 1914 1915 1916 1917

■Wright brothers make first powered flight

■Russo-Japanese War begins

■*The Psychopathology of Everyday Life* (Freud)

■Irish Sinn Fein created

■Einstein formulates Theory of Relativity

■British Labour Party established

■Earthquake hits San Francisco

Boy Scouts founded ■

Taft elected U.S. president ■

Ford opens first auto assembly line ■

■Wilson elected U.S. president

■S.S. *Titanic* sinks

■Girl Scouts founded

■WWI begins

■Panama Canal opens

■German sub sinks *Lusitania*

First birth control clinic opened ■

Czar abdicates after ■ Russian Revolution

■"Pomp and Circumstance" (Elgar)

■Enrico Caruso's first record

■*Peter Rabbit* (Potter)

■*The Great Train Robbery* film (Porter)

■*Man and Superman* (Shaw)

■*The Call of the Wild* (London)

■*The Cherry Orchard* (Chekhov)

■*Peter Pan* (Barrie)

■First movies at Pittsburgh nickelodeon

■Ziegfeld Follies

■*Ballets Russes* (Diaghilev)

■*Howard's End* (Forster)

■*Naughty Marietta* (Herbert)

■*Der Rosenkavalier* (R. Strauss)

■"Alexander's Ragtime Band" (Berlin)

■*Le Sacre du Printemps* (Stravinsky)

■*Sons and Lovers* (Lawrence)

"Over There" ■ (Cohan)

■Deanery Garden (Lutyens)

Hampstead Garden ■ Suburb (Parker and Unwin)

Robie House (Wright) ■

Gamble House (Greene and Greene) ■

Forest Hills Gardens (Olmsted, Jr.) ■

Harlequin (Picasso) ■

Craftsman Farms (Stickley) ■

Hôtel Guimard (Guimard) ■

First Church of ■ Christ, Scientist (Maybeck)

■Finnish National Museum (Saarinen et al.)

■Purcell House (Purcell and Elmslie)

■Grove Park Inn (Seely)

La Jolla Women's Club (Gill) ■

Panama-Pacific Exposition, ■ San Francisco

Matthewson House ■ (Maybeck)

1902 1903 1904 1905 1906 1907 1908 1909 1910 1911 1912 1913 1914 1915 1916 1917

A NEW MIDDLE CLASS

As the twentieth century dawned, people were beginning to drift toward cities and suburbs, away from the wholesome country life prescribed by earlier social reformers. By 1900 almost as many American men worked in factories as in fields. Rapid-transit systems linked urban areas, while residential suburbs grew along with the electric trolley lines and interurban trains. The nascent automobile industry promised even greater mobility.

Most women still worked at home as housewives—and sometimes as pieceworkers in cottage industries—but opportunities for outside employment increased as offices and factories sought to fill secretarial and assembly-line positions, albeit at low wages. For the first time, children of both sexes were able to attend public schools, and women could teach in them.

Industrial society and capitalism allowed a few of its most enterprising members to amass fabulous wealth, but it also favored the rapid growth of the middle class. Houses were smaller, but more families owned one. As overcrowded tenements were gradually reformed, apartments, once the resort of the downwardly mobile and the down-and-out, became a standard of urban life.

Lord Armstrong, an armaments manufacturer, enjoyed the good life at Cragside (1870–84, Richard Norman Shaw) in Northumberland. An elaborate hearth and stained glass by Morris and Company added the perfect period touches to his inglenook.

Signs of Home for the New Middle Class

Small house, often owner occupied

No separate entrance hall or parlor

Inglenook

Compact kitchen

Work-saving surfaces (tile, linoleum, enamel paint)

Few servants, many appliances

One-car garage

Women found ready outlets for their creative skills at places such as Rookwood Pottery in Cincinnati, founded by Maria Longworth Nichols in 1880.

... to be counted off into a heap of mechanism, numbered with its wheels, and weighed with its hammer strokes,—this nature bade not,— God blesses not— this humanity for no long time is able to endure.
—John Ruskin,
The Stones of Venice,
1851–53

As the uglier effects of capitalism, industrialization, and urbanization made themselves apparent, society was pressed to ease the burdens of workers and the poor. England legalized labor unions and gave the vote to working-class males. The influx of nearly 10.5 million immigrants into the United States between 1905 and 1914 led to a housing crisis that resulted in tenement reforms and the establishment of company housing.

Strides were made on the road to suffrage for women, as "new women" of the 1890s contended for enfranchisement. More women were leaving home—not just for art classes, club meetings, and tea parties but also for business, school, and college. Even fashion reflected growing independence, as bustles and corsets gave way to less restrictive dress with slightly shorter (although sometimes hobbled) skirts.

"Jim Crow" laws of the late 1800s pushed civil rights for minority races and ethnic groups far into the future, but some schools and colleges for blacks were created. Estate taxes in Great Britain and the income tax in the United States spread the wealth, and the merits of socialism, communism, and capitalism were debated at every level of society.

ART IN CRAFT

Out of the Gothic Revival movement, which preached a return to honest handcraftsmanship, arose an abhorrence of meaningless ornament. It was joined by a revolt against machine-generated excesses in art, architecture, and daily life. From England and the Continent came a cry for an aesthetic suited to the age, not an architectural or decorative "style" but a new approach to living and working in the late nineteenth century—a joyful union of art and craft.

The Arts and Crafts ideal of simple, handcrafted comfort is seen in William Morris's Red House (1859, Philip Webb) in Bexleyheath, Kent.

From the 1860s until World War I, the ideas of Arts and Crafts proponent William Morris found sympathetic followers in Germany, Austria, Belgium, Holland, Scandinavia, and America. All were eager to abandon Victorian frippery for simple lines and honest materials, well proportioned and impeccably crafted.

Although England led the movement, each nation molded Arts and Crafts concepts in its own image. British architects sought inspiration in the small buildings of medieval villages, the "Cotswold cottage" stripped to its Gothic bones. Americans incorporated Colonial Revival elements, while Scandinavians rediscovered the colors and shapes of traditional folk painting. Rather than revive past styles, Arts and Crafts designers made knowing use of historic forms for contemporary ends. Large or small, these buildings were informal, generally asymmetrical, and, at least in intent, functional.

Several new forms flourished in America: the bungalow, a low-slung, deep-eaved American reinvention of an Eastern phenomenon; the Prairie School house, whose horizontal lines headed for the future; and the Craftsman house, popularized through Gustav Stickley's magazine, *The Craftsman.*

Green Gables (1911, Greene and Greene), Woodside, California (opposite), simulated the thatched roof of an English cottage. Houses from Stickley (below) were more modest.

When a style is found to be original and vital it is a certainty that it has sprung from the needs of the plain people. . . .
—Gustav Stickley, *Craftsman Homes,* 2d ed., 1909

ARTS AND CRAFTS FEATURES

Plans: Center-hall plan (Craftsman and vernacular houses) or informal, somewhat asymmetrical and picturesque (architect-designed houses), with open floor plans or large openings between rooms, some (especially Prairie houses) with large, glazed doors.

Materials: Regional materials, especially wood, brick, and stucco and sometimes local stone; roman brick (Prairie houses); half-timbered effect (English and Craftsman houses).

Colors: Muted earth tones with color accents: deep reds, browns, greens, and blues.

Roofs: High front or side gables (English houses); broad, low, front-facing gables (bungalows); flat roofs (Prairie School); deep, open eaves, sometimes with strut supports, especially in American bungalows and Prairie houses; slate or shingle coverings preferred.

Doors: Large and prominent but not ornamented; nontraditional paneling and glazing, sometimes with stained or beveled glass.

Windows: Large; grouped and ribbon windows, bays, and oriels; some casements but usually double-hung sash; "cottage sash"; multiple small panes over a large single pane.

Porches: Entrance porches, not full-width verandas; sleeping porches; pergolas, porte-cochères, and terraces; screened living and eating porches.

Ornamentation: Mostly in structural features, such as patterned brick-work (English houses), chimneys, and shaped eave supports (bunga-lows and Prairie houses); some decorative terra-cotta plaques and metal hardware.

From Morris's Red House (1859), Bexley-heath, Kent, to the Irwin House (1906, Greene and Greene), Pasadena, California, the English and American Arts and Crafts had as many differences as similarities.

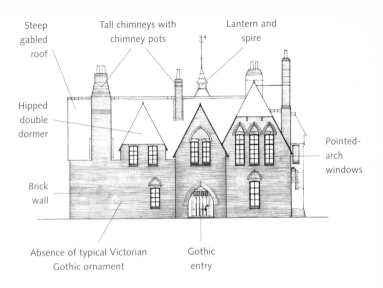

Steep gabled roof

Tall chimneys with chimney pots

Lantern and spire

Hipped double dormer

Pointed-arch windows

Brick wall

Absence of typical Victorian Gothic ornament

Gothic entry

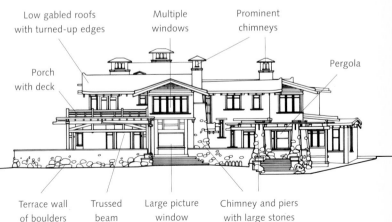

Low gabled roofs with turned-up edges

Multiple windows

Prominent chimneys

Porch with deck

Pergola

Terrace wall of boulders

Trussed beam

Large picture window

Chimney and piers with large stones

At Hill House (1904), Helensburgh, Scotland, Mackintosh created a totally unified environment based on the square. His designs were more stylized than other Arts and Crafts work, but he shared an affinity for the organic approach.

Craftsman Associations

Century Guild, England (1882)

Art Workers Guild, England (1884)

Guild of Handicraft, England (1888)

Roycroft Community, East Aurora, New York (1893)

Society of Arts and Crafts, Boston (1897)

Wiener Werkstätte, Vienna (1903)

Deutsche Werkbund, Germany (1907)

In calling for national and regional building forms that drew on historic vernacular precedents, William Morris's powerful voice was joined by many others. Prominent English Arts and Crafts architects included C. F. A. Voysey, M. H. Baillie Scott, C. R. Ashbee, and W. R. Lethaby. British and Scottish designers such as Charles Rennie Mackintosh stressed beautiful materials and exquisite finishes rather than ornament. In Austria, Josef Hoffmann and Joseph Maria Olbrich approached building design in a similar fashion. France and Belgium contributed a related but separate design impetus, Art Nouveau, using sensuous curves, not straight lines.

Preeminent among Arts and Crafts architects in the United States were Charles and Henry Greene, Wilson Eyre, Bernard Maybeck, and Frank Lloyd Wright. American crafts communities like Elbert Hubbard's Roycrofters sprang up, and popular magazines such as Gustav Stickley's *The Craftsman* made Arts and Crafts ideas broadly accessible.

Among landscape architects, England's Gertrude Jekyll worked hand-in-hand with architects like Edwin Lutyens, while planners strove to beautify entire cities and build garden communities for the working class.

MOVEMENT LEADERS

**Edward William Bok
(1863–1930)**
Editor, *Ladies' Home Journal*
(1889–1919);
Sponsor, Rose Valley
Community, Pa. (1901)

**Elbert G. Hubbard
(1856–1915)**
Founder, Roycroft Community
(1893), East Aurora, N.Y.

W. R. Lethaby (1857–1931)
Founder, Art Workers Guild
(1884);
Architect, Avon Tyrell (1893),
Hampshire;
Codirector, Central School of
Arts and Crafts (1896–1911),
London

**Henry Chapman Mercer
(1856–1930)**
Historian, collector, ceramicist;
Founder, Moravian Pottery
and Tile Works (1898), Doylestown, Pa.

William Morris (1834–96)
Designer, social reformer, poet;
Founder, Morris and Company
(1861), London;
Publisher, Kelmscott Press
(1891–97)

John Ruskin (1819–1900)
Social and art critic, author;
*The Seven Lamps of Archi-
tecture* (1849–51);
The Stones of Venice (1851–53)

Gustav Stickley (1858–1942)
Founder, Craftsman Workshops
(1899);
Publisher, *The Craftsman*
magazine (1901–16);
Author, *Craftsman Homes*,
2d ed. (1909);
Designer, Craftsman Farms
(1910), Morris Plains, N.J.

ARCHITECTS

C. R. Ashbee (1863–1942)
38–39 Cheyne Walk (1901),
London

Wilson Eyre (1858–1944)
University of Pennsylvania
Museum (1893–1926, with
others), Philadelphia

Edmund Gilchrist (1885–1953)
Lincoln Drive Development
(1910–21, with others),
Philadelphia

Irving Gill (1870–1936)
La Jolla Women's Club (1914),
La Jolla, Calif.

**Charles Sumner Greene
(1868–1957) and Henry
Mather Greene (1870–1954)**
Blacker House (1907),
Pasadena, Calif.;
Gamble House (1909),
Pasadena, Calif.

**Walter Burley Griffin
(1876–1937) and Marion
Mahony Griffin (1871–1962)**
Rock Crest–Rock Glen (1912),
Mason City, Iowa

**Edwin Landseer Lutyens
(1869–1944)**
Goddards (1899), Dorking,
Surrey;
Little Thakeham (1902),
Storrington, West Sussex

**Charles Rennie Mackintosh
(1868–1928)**
Hill House (1904),
Helensburgh, Scotland;
Glasgow School of Art (1909),
Scotland

**Arthur Heygate Mackmurdo
(1851–1942)**
25 Cadogan Gardens (1899),
London

Bernard Maybeck (1862–1957)
First Church of Christ, Scientist
(1911), Berkeley, Calif.

Julia Morgan (1872–1957)
St. John's Presbyterian Church
(1910), Berkeley, Calif.

**Joseph Maria Olbrich
(1867–1908)**
Austellungshaus der Wiener
Sezession (1898), Vienna

**Barry Parker (1867–1947) and
Raymond Unwin (1863–1946)**
Hampstead Garden Suburb
(1906), London

Bruce Price (1845–1903)
Tuxedo Park, N.Y. (1890)

William Price (1861–1916)
Founder, Rose Valley
Community, Pa. (1901)

Eliel Saarinen (1873–1950)
Finnish National Museum
(1912), Helsinki

**M. H. Baillie Scott
(1865–1945)**
Waterlow Court (1909),
Hampstead, London

C. F. A. Voysey (1857–1941)
Foster House (1891), Bedford
Park, London;
The Orchard (1899), Chorley
Wood, Hertfordshire

Philip Webb (1831–1915)
William Morris's Red House
(1859), Bexleyheath, Kent;
Standen (1894), East Grinstead,
West Sussex

**Frank Lloyd Wright
(1867–1959)**
Martin House (1904),
Buffalo, N.Y.

CITY PLANNERS

Ebenezer Howard (1850–1928)
Bournville, England (1898);
Garden Cities of Tomorrow
(1902)

John Nolen (1869–1937)
Kingsport, Tenn. (1921);
Venice, Fla. (1925)

LANDSCAPE ARCHITECTS

Gertrude Jekyll (1843–1932)
Munstead Wood Garden
(1896), Surrey;
Goddards Garden (1899),
Dorking, Surrey;
Hestercombe Garden (1906),
Somerset

Jens Jensen (1860–1951)
Chicago park system
(1906–18);
Fair Lane (1920), Dearborn,
Mich.

**Frederick Law Olmsted, Jr.
(1870–1957)**
Forest Hills Gardens (1909),
Queens, N.Y.;
Palos Verdes Estates (1923),
Los Angeles, Calif.

ILLUSTRATORS

**Aubrey V. Beardsley
(1872–98)**
Book and poster illustration;
Drawings for Oscar Wilde's
Salome (1894)

Will H. Bradley (1868–1962)
Posters and illustrations;
The Chapbook illustrations
(1894); *Bradley, His Book*
(1896)

DESIGNERS

Walter Crane (1845–1915)
Wallpaper and book designs

Harvey Ellis (1852–1904)
Building and furniture designs
for Stickley

**Margaret Macdonald
(1865–1933) and Frances
Macdonald (1874–1921)**
Interior design

**George Mann Niedecken
(1878–1945)**
Furniture and interiors for
Wright and Prairie School
architects

**Louis Comfort Tiffany
(1848–1933)**
Founder, Tiffany Studios and
Tiffany and Company (1879)

Candace Wheeler (1827–1923)
Founder, New York Society
of Decorative Arts (1877);
Principles of Home Decoration
(1903)

ARTISANS

**Sidney Barnsley (1865–1926)
and Ernest Barnsley
(1863–1926)**
Craft Workshop at Sapperton

**Ernest Allen Batchelder
(1875–1957)**
Ceramics;
Writer and educator

**William De Morgan
(1839–1917)**
Ceramics for Morris

**Arthur Wesley Dow
(1857–1922)**
Paintings and ceramics

**William Henry Grueby
(1867–1925)**
Founder, Grueby Faience
Company (1897)

Dard Hunter (1883–1966)
Book, furniture, and glass
designs for Roycroft Shops

Georg Jensen (1866–1935)
Silverwork

John La Farge (1835–1910)
Stained glass

**Charles P. Limbert
(1854–1923)**
Furniture

**John Gardner Low
(1835–1907)**
Founder, J. and G. Low Art Tile
Works (1877), Chelsea, Mass.

**Mary Louise McLaughlin
(1847–1939)**
Founder, Cincinnati Pottery
Club (1879)

May Morris (1862–1938)
Weaving and embroidery

**Maria Longworth Nichols
(1849–1932)**
Founder, Rookwood Pottery
(1880)

**Adelaide Alsop Robineau
(1865–1929)**
Editor, *Keramic Studio*

Charles Rohlfs (1853–1936)
Furniture

Dirk Van Erp (1859–1933)
Lamps and metalwork

Samuel Yellin (1885–1940)
Metalwork

Although there was no single Arts and Crafts style, the movement was committed to utility as well as unity between a building and its site and with nature itself. Local materials were used simply and picturesquely, and regional, ethnic, historic, and folk traditions—English brick-and-timber Cotswold cottages, southwestern American adobe missions, and Finnish log houses—were incorporated into designs that honored the past while serving the present.

A large Swiss chalet, Sagamore (1899, William Durant) is one of the great camps of the Adirondacks. Owner Alfred Vanderbilt sits at right in the sled.

Roofs were commonly gabled, although Frank Lloyd Wright and the Prairie School architects used both gabled and flat forms; Irving Gill's modern California pueblos had flat roofs. Steep gables recalled eighteenth-century precedents, while low, hipped roofs evoked the Cotswold cottage. Large, low-swooping, gabled roofs and deep front porches defined the bungalow. Projecting eaves with exposed rafters and triangular timber struts were frequent in Craftsman houses, bungalows, and the California work of Greene and Greene and Bernard Maybeck.

Often a mix of brick, stone, stucco, and wood enlivened walls paneled with boards imitating the timber frames of folk houses.

All types of windows—double-hung sash, casements, sidelights and transoms, bay windows, and oriels—were used. Small leaded panes over a single pane were known as "cottage sash." Strip and corner windows were common, especially in Prairie buildings. Glazed doors, often with patterned or stained glass, were fashionable.

Pergolas and sleeping porches were essential, while porte-cochères and garages announced the automobile age.

With steeply sloping roofs and tall chimneys, the Barn (1896, Edward Schroder Prior), Exmouth, England, is one of the most expansive country houses of the Arts and Crafts era.

Period designers built tall, picturesque chimneys of stone or brick, often drawing on earlier styles.

Liberty and Company of London, opened by Arthur Lasenby Liberty in 1875, was a great Arts and Crafts success story. Part of its new building complex (1925, E.T. and E. S. Hall) invoked Tudor precursors with a half-timbered facade. The interior recycled the remains of two men-of-war.

[Find] the best stone, make the best brick, forge the best iron, cut the best timber, so season and dress and build as will make the best construction.
—Edward Schroder Prior, *Architectural Review,* 1901

Honest materials, honestly treated, were the hallmark of Arts and Crafts architecture. The selection was based on local and historical usage. English architects particularly delighted in combining colored or textured building materials, such as pebbles and local stone, or creating patterned brick walls.

The bungalow, a favorite Arts and Crafts building type, came in wood (shingles or clapboard) or local stone, even cobblestone. Brick was a common choice for English buildings; in the eastern United States it appeared as well on English colonial and picturesque, European-inspired examples. Prairie houses like Frank Lloyd Wright's often used narrow roman brick in buff or earth tones.

Stucco walls became stylish for Pueblo, Spanish Colonial Revival, Craftsman, and Prairie School houses and for half-timbered, Old English—style buildings. The new reinforced concrete was valued for its fireproof characteristics, especially in low-cost housing experiments such as Thomas Edison's design used at Ingersoll Terrace (1917), Union, New Jersey. Hollow-clay structural tile and cast-cement blocks with plain or decorative finish were used for houses and decorative terra cotta and cast stone for larger buildings.

ORNAMENT

On the polychrome ceramic facade of the Everard Printing Works (1901, W. J. Neatby), Bristol, figures representing Gutenberg and Morris flank the Spirit of Literature. Owner Edward Everard wanted his building to serve as a memorial to old and new masters of the art of printing.

Decorative Devices

Prominent door and
  window hardware
  of iron, bronze,
  or copper
Picturesque chimneys
Generous roof
  overhangs with
  open eaves
Stained glass
Terra-cotta wall
  ornament

Except when it formed an integral part of the structure, ornament was not prominent in Arts and Crafts buildings and objects. Designers rejected not only Victorian decoration but also classical ornament, which they considered imitative, boring, and irrelevant to modern life.

Their emphasis lay instead on picturesque massing, fine materials, and careful finishing. Craftsman buildings in particular shunned decoration. The California houses by Greene and Greene exemplify the Arts and Crafts reliance on the expressive use of beautiful materials, especially shaped timbers, to replace formal ornament.

Stained glass was a common exception to the dislike of ornament, and designers such as Frank Lloyd Wright, Louis Tiffany, and John La Farge often turned colored light to decorative effect. Hardware, particularly revivals of medieval strap hingework, provided another notable Arts and Crafts touch. It was heavy, handwrought, and beautifully designed.

Decorative wall panels of terra cotta in naturalistic, sinuous forms were also used. Often, however, chimneys and the roof structure were the most ornamental aspects of an Arts and Crafts building.

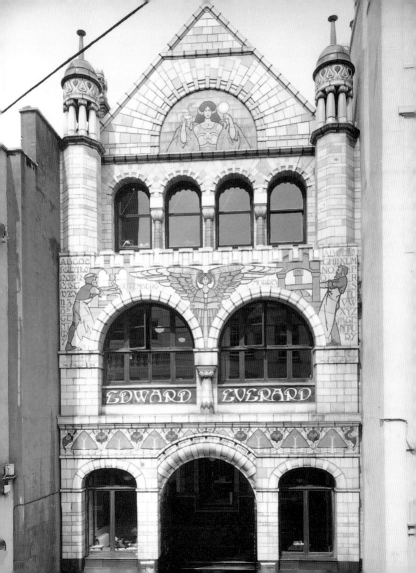

EDWARD EVERARD

Never had landscape and building been so closely allied. Arts and Crafts architects and landscape gardeners worked together to create "organic" compositions in which buildings seemed to grow out of their sites. Porches and large windows encouraged easy movement between house and garden.

The accoutrements of the classical, formal garden were discarded for picturesque, naturalistic settings featuring rustic, vine-covered pergolas and outdoor "rooms" with garden furniture built of gnarled tree branches, designed to encourage quiet contemplation.

On a livelier note, the cottage garden, popularized by Gertrude Jekyll, was a seemingly rampant display of flowers, shrubbery, and trees. The physical and spiritual benefits of outdoor exercise and fresh air were stressed, and more homeowners became gardeners, abetted by popular magazines such as *House and Garden*. Even estates were landscaped in naturalistic designs using native plants.

Urban parks continued to develop under the influence of designers such as Frederick Law Olmsted, Sr. and Jr., and Jens Jensen. In the United States the growth of the national park system was entirely in keeping with the back-to-nature outlook of the era.

"What he builds seems to grow out of the ground," said the landscape architect Gertrude Jekyll of Edwin Lutyens, the architect of Munstead Wood (1896), her home in Surrey. Local sandstone and traditional building methods proved a felicitous match for the carefully plotted, harmonious colors in Jekyll's "natural" garden.

I try for beauty and harmony everywhere, especially for harmony of color.
—Gertrude Jekyll,
Wood and Garden, 1904

INSIDE

The most telling Arts and Crafts features were inside: in layouts, fittings, and finishes. House plans were open and spacious, often on a single floor to minimize housekeeping burdens. A generous combination hall and living area encouraged family togetherness and brought visitors quickly into the family orbit. Gleaming woods, textured surfaces, handwoven and embroidered textiles, and mellow colors warmed the Arts and Crafts building.

A light screen between inside and out, the oak-motif entrance of the Gamble House (1909), Pasadena, California, was the work of Charles Sumner Greene.

Down to its hooded fireplace with tile facing, the Hawley House (c. 1900), Baltimore, presented a model Mission interior. In American Craftsman houses, aphorisms or homilies spelled out in Old English lettering were often incised on copper fireplace hoods or carved above doors or on mantelpieces.

The love you liberate in your work is the love you keep.
—Door carving, Roycroft Salon, Roycroft Inn (1903), East Aurora, New York

Materials that were chosen for their inherent beauty and appropriateness, finished "truthfully and with great care," defined the Arts and Crafts interior. The movement's interest in indigenous architecture carried over to a preference for using local materials whenever possible, inside as well as out.

Painted plaster walls frequently were textured or accented by wood strips directing the eye. Woodwork was rarely painted and was generally neither stained nor heavily varnished. Staircases were massive, paneled constructions of squared newels and balusters in natural wood. Oak was a particularly favored wood, considered an appropriately "masculine" choice for the Arts and Crafts building. Veneers, varnishes, and faux finishes were scorned.

Large fireplaces, commonly with inglenook seating areas, also served as a design focus. The hearth, in fact, was viewed as an aesthetic and social necessity, sacred to the celebration of life and family. Mantels and fireplaces were of wood and rough stone or brick, with ceramic-tiled fireplace surrounds and, perhaps, copper hoods. Sometimes a simple shelf replaced the elaborate mantel ensembles of former years.

Textured, painted walls in creamy tones or quiet, earthy colors were generally preferred, but not all Arts and Crafts practitioners were negative toward wallpaper.

William Morris himself designed many papers for Arts and Crafts buildings—mostly because he could find nothing on the market that met his design criteria. Today his abstract leafy and nature-inspired patterns are almost as popular as they were in the nineteenth century.

Christopher Dresser, the noted designer whose opinions influenced interiors for many years, insisted that wallpaper should be restricted to flat patterns in one or two not-too-bright colors and should feature repetitions of a single geometric design "powdered" (evenly distributed) over a solid ground. Scenic friezes were popular: Arthurian knights for dining areas and fairy-tale characters for children's rooms, in charming papers by such noted book illustrators as Walter Crane and Kate Greenaway.

Handwoven, wall-hung tapestries were highly valued during the period. William Morris's designs based on chivalric legends were in great demand among those who could afford them.

Morris and Dresser parted company when it came to wallpapers. Morris's Green Dining Room (1867) for the South Kensington Museum (now the Victoria and Albert Museum) recalls a woody arbor, every inch filled with leafy splendors.

I must confess that I am not very fond of wall-papers under any circumstances. I prefer a tinted or painted wall....
—Christopher Dresser, *Principles of Decorative Design*, 1873

INSIDE

Arts and Crafts designers were adamant on this point: realistic, three-dimensional flowers and vines had no business growing underfoot in any well-designed home. Nor was riotous color acceptable on floors. Much better were calmly colored, plain or all-over abstract designs understandable from any direction.

Indefatigable in his zeal for providing good design, William Morris produced handwoven floor carpets through his firm, Morris and Company. Louis Tiffany and his Associated Artists, which included Candace Wheeler, also turned out handmade carpets.

The era was a grand time for "good" wooden floors, carefully polished but not highly varnished. Antique oriental rugs for them were much admired, although they were far beyond the budgets of most households; true Arts and Crafters scorned machine-made imitations. Navajo rugs were favored by Americans. Custom-crafted rugs for specific houses fit the Arts and Crafts precept of unity of architecture and decoration, a virtue at which Frank Lloyd Wright excelled in his Prairie houses.

Henry Mercer's Moravian Pottery and Tile Works made many story-telling mosaic tiles such as "Reaping with a Sickle."

Decorator and Furnisher magazine in 1886 recommended this geometrically patterned wooden flooring. Elsewhere, ceramic-tiled bathroom floors and linoleum, cork, or rubber flooring in the kitchen eased the housework chores.

The 1888 catalogue of the J. L. Mott Iron Works in New York offered the latest in household plumbing: an oval-bowl water closet (above) and the "most complete Bath, combining Needle, Spray, Shower, Liver Spray and Douche" (opposite).

Arts and Crafts buildings, especially in the United States, benefited not so much from the invention of modern miracles as from the refinement of those already at hand.

Electricity and its attendant marvels—lighting fixtures, electric stoves, chafing dishes, toasters, saucepans, and even hair-curling irons—transformed the domestic scene into something recognizably close to what we know today, despite unwieldy knob-and-tube wiring.

For one thing, there was likely to be (at least in the United States) a source of running water everywhere it was needed, in both baths and kitchens—and, pretty much on demand, it was hot water. Drainage systems in most cities and even small towns could be relied on to carry water and wastes away from the house without poisoning the inhabitants, and bathrooms had sanitary porcelain tubs, basins, and toilets.

Gas lines brought a clean, quick means of heat to a large number of residences, and some affluent households even had large, gas-heated, upright clothes dryers. Air conditioning and electric or gas refrigerators were still years away, but ice was available to most people for relatively little cost or effort.

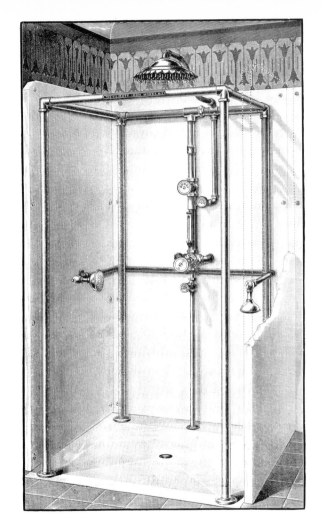

INSIDE

FINISHING TOUCHES

Every Arts and Crafts architect's fantasy was to be commissioned by a wealthy client both to design and to furnish an entire house, from sofas, tables, and chairs to tablecloths, wine glasses, candlesticks, rugs, curtains, and art. It seldom happened, as most clients held firmly to some cherished pieces. When the fantasy did materialize, the result could be a glorious expression of an individual designer's vision of beauty: simple, functional, and unified in theme.

Greene and Greene's artistry was evident even in the early Reeve House (1904), Long Beach, California. A built-in curio cabinet frames the cozy inglenook.

*My early approach
to the chair was
something between
contempt and
desperation. . . .
All my life my legs
have been banged
up somewhere
by the chairs I have
designed.*
—Frank Lloyd Wright,
The Natural House,
1954

Under the Arts and Crafts influence, furniture lost its curving lines and most of its applied ornament and carving. Oak—native, inexpensive, and innocent of paint, stain, or glossy varnish—often replaced imported woods. Pegged and dovetailed joints edged out cheaper construction methods.

American markets were flooded with furnishings from Gustav Stickley and his siblings' companies, as well as other firms such as Limbert. These blocky pieces were often called Mission because they were thought to be inspired by the furnishings of Spanish colonial churches and because they honestly bespoke their purpose, or mission.

Charles Rennie Mackintosh's more linear chairs were echoed across the Atlantic by those of George Niedecken, who designed furnishings for Frank Lloyd Wright's houses. Even Wright sometimes used Craftsman chairs: clients may well have blessed the capacious upholstered seats after trying Wright's straight, narrow ones.

To offset any feeling of severity created by all-wood interiors and furnishings, Arts and Crafts rooms frequently contained simple, straight-lined, woven willow chairs and settees in soft, natural greenish tones. The charm of willow pieces, according to Stickley, was that they were purely and obviously handcrafted, whereas elaborate rattan pieces might look too much like factory work.

The Craftsman, Stickley's magazine, encouraged homeowners to make their own wooden settles, benches, tables, chairs, and footstools. Meanwhile, the British stuck to their guns on handcraftsmanship, relegating Arts and Crafts design to the province of the wealthy and well educated.

Greene and Greene's living room table (opposite) for the Blacker House (1907) featured "dancing" ebony peg joinery. The familiar Morris chair (below) symbolized the homey comfort desired by Arts and Crafts designers.

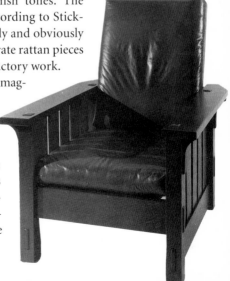

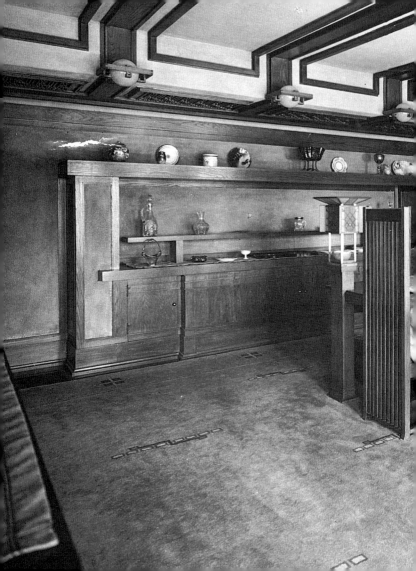

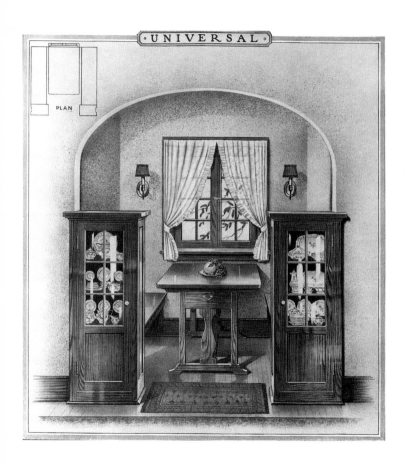

BUILT-INS

Arts and Crafts architects eager to ensure total design unity in their clients' homes frequently turned to built-in furnishings. High-style houses, such as Greene and Greene's "ultimate" California bungalows and Frank Lloyd Wright's Prairie houses, featured custom-designed, handcrafted masterpieces of fine joinery in rare woods.

Homelier bungalows and Four Squares received built-in furnishings of inexpensive oak or pine, vastly increasing a house's comfort quotient with stock millwork components. Almost any amenity could be ordered by catalogue and delivered to the building site, from inglenooks to breakfast nooks to "cozy corners." Sears, Roebuck's 1910 *Special Catalogue for Homebuilders,* for example, offered a full line of built-ins in a variety of styles, including a Mission sideboard and a Craftsman china closet and buffet. Throughout the nation wholesale millwork companies distributed their catalogues to local dealers and lumber yards, providing easy access to sought-after pieces.

Built-ins became more than mere furnishings. They were part of the architecture—allowing a fully integrated and economical approach to the business of living.

Cozy breakfast nooks became a stock built-in item, some of them complete with pull-down seats or attached china cabinets.

Built-ins by Mail

Buffets with mirrors
    and art-glass doors

Glass-front bookcases

Window seats

Sideboards

Room dividers

Decorative screens

Kitchen cabinets

Wardrobes

Linen cases

Hideaway ironing
    boards

To enhance the dining experience in his Robie House (1908), Chicago, Wright created a room within a room, lighted by built-in fixtures (pages 52–53).

In addition to designing fabrics such as "Brother Rabbit" (opposite), Morris taught himself tapestry weaving and embroidery. His daughter May (to his left below, c. 1865) was a prominent embroiderer.

Handweaving, largely abandoned with the industrial revolution, made a stunning comeback in the Arts and Crafts period. Table covers, curtains, upholstery fabrics, tapestries, and carpets took on new importance as part of a well-integrated decorating scheme.

Although most weaving was still carried out in factories, the textile arts were activities in which women could shine without abandoning domesticity—an important consideration in a society not yet disabused of the Victorian view of perfect, unworldly womanhood. Influential males such as William Morris also acknowledged the importance of textile design and manufacture.

Needlework of all sorts was elevated from mere "fancy work" to a serious art form at craft centers such as Haslemere Peasant Industries and Candace Wheeler's workshops. Themes and patterns were drawn from folk traditions, regional crafts, oriental designs, and Native American motifs. Simple, widely spaced, repetitive designs came from nature but were not naturalistic. Background colors were often textured but quiet-colored, while designs were picked out in vibrant hues.

Don't think too much of style.
—William Morris, lecture on art, 1881

Unlike Wright, Tiffany liked leaded-glass windows that filled rooms with explicit depictions of nature. Tiffany Studios produced this daffodil design around 1910.

[By] chipping the glass in such a way as to give irregular faceted surfaces, . . . a material was obtained which rivaled the painter's palette in its range of tones and eclipsed the iridescence and brilliance of Roman and Egyptian glass. . . .
—Louis Tiffany,
The Forum, July 1893

Simple, window-length curtains fit the mood of Arts and Crafts rooms better than heavy, ornate draperies. The less formal lifestyle demanded the end of elaborate folds, multi-layered window treatments, and fussy lambrequins, all of which were viewed as degenerate Victorian concessions to the female taste. So did the era's emphasis on sunlight, fresh air, and outside views. Curtain rods, although often visible and ornamental, were unashamedly functional. Window fabrics, preferably handwoven, gained interest from their texture and from borders or panels of embroidery.

A widespread interest in stained glass for houses as well as for churches kept glassmakers and designers such as Louis Tiffany and John La Farge busy with beautiful, richly colored patterns derived from nature or taken from mythology. Architects liked to embellish their buildings with their own stained-glass work. Greene and Greene provided the stunning tree design for the front door of the Gamble House (1909) in Pasadena, California. Frank Lloyd Wright, as usual, had his own ideas about the proper decoration of glass, preferring flat, geometric designs that would not compete with the view.

LIGHTING AND LAMPS

As the twentieth century approached, electricity gradually overtook the gaslight era. By World War I electric lighting was the rule in urban houses and businesses in the United States, although many rural areas had to make do with less-modern alternatives. The day of the massive chandelier had passed.

Electric floor lamps and table lamps were popular ways to provide portable lighting, but architects and designers generally preferred built-in or wall-mounted lights, such as wall sconces, to maintain design control over the entire setting. Central ceiling-mounted electric lights were liable to be, at best, awkward and unattractive contrivances, but overhead illumination and decorative unity could be provided by placing wall-mounted fixtures high on the walls or on ceiling beams.

The ultimate lamplighter of the Arts and Crafts era in the United States was Louis Tiffany, who provided wealthy clients with brilliant stained-glass lampshades, often with an Art Nouveau flair. Dirk Van Erp, a Dutch-born California metal artisan, specialized in hammered-copper lamp shades. Not surprisingly, many artisans of the period preferred to design candlesticks and candelabra—relics from an earlier time.

Rectilinear lights were popular, from simple table lamps to an elaborate copper-and-silver hanging lantern (c. 1906, Dard Hunter) for the Roycroft Inn, East Aurora, New York.

Take the train for East Aurory, Where we work for Art and Glory.
—Felix Shay, *Elbert Hubbard of East Aurora*, 1926

FINE ARTS

Among the most familiar and evocative images of the early Arts and Crafts period are Dante Gabriel Rossetti's romantic portraits of William Morris's dark-haired wife, Jane Burden. She was his Beatrice in *The Saluta-tion of Beatrice* (1882).

Preoccupied with legendary themes from the Middle Ages, Pre-Raphaelite artists pre-saged many of the ideas that held sway in the passage from Impressionism to Post-Impressionism. Later paintings in realistic settings—for example, *The Artist's Mother* (1871), by James MacNeill Whistler—de-parted markedly from the preferred roman-ticism. John Ruskin's outraged response to one Whistler landscape resulted in a bitter lawsuit.

The influence of oriental art, particularly Japanese and Chinese painting and prints, was evident in the work of many artists, such as Mary Cassatt, whose paintings fo-cused on intimate yet unsentimental por-traits of mothers and children.

Above all other forms, illustrative art defined the Arts and Crafts approach to painting, as the line between art and craft, utility and aesthetics, became increasingly blurred. Posters, books, and magazines made frequent and innovative use of color lithog-raphy and pen-and-ink drawings by artists such as Howard Pyle. The development of original color art prints, in which production was personally overseen by the artist, was a major extension of the fine arts repertoire.

Popular Paintings

The Sleeping Knights
    (1871, Edward
    Burne-Jones)
The Laidly Worm
    (1881, Walter Crane)
*Isabella, or, the Pot
    of Basil* (1897, John
    White Alexander)

The Arts and Crafts years were perhaps the most fertile time for printing and publishing and all their related artistic activities. Like the illuminated manuscripts of medieval days, book binding and book production became an art that unified form and substance: literary content, illustrations, and covers. Small printing houses from William

Morris's Kelmscott Press to Elbert Hubbard's Roycroft Press expressed their individuality with richly tooled and gilded leather book covers, handmade papers, careful typography, meticulous printing, and a wealth of illustrations, often in color.

Morris lent his considerable skills to illustrate *The Works of Geoffrey Chaucer* in 1896, a Kelmscott Press book that rivaled handcrafted illuminated manuscripts.

The advent of color printing allowed advertising art, color illustrations in books and magazines, and poster art to blossom, giving employment to artists such as Henri de Toulouse-Lautrec in France, Aubrey Beardsley in England, and N. C. Wyeth and Will Bradley in the United States. Illustrated book covers by artists such as Margaret Armstrong and Louis Rhead became almost the rule. In the United States, Boston was a center for the revival of fine printing and book design.

Will Bradley's poster of "The Kiss," publicizing *Bradley, His Book* (1896), shows the diverse sources of the illustrator's work: medieval, Art Nouveau, and Arts and Crafts.

ART POTTERY

Pottery came glazed, such as this Rookwood vase (1909, Charles Schmidt), or in earthen finishes: a teapot (1905–11) from Clifton.

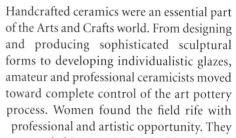

Handcrafted ceramics were an essential part of the Arts and Crafts world. From designing and producing sophisticated sculptural forms to developing individualistic glazes, amateur and professional ceramicists moved toward complete control of the art pottery process. Women found the field rife with professional and artistic opportunity. They were led in America by the likes of Adelaide Alsop Robineau, editor of *Keramic Studio*, Mary Louise McLaughlin, and Maria Longworth Nichols and their counterparts in England, such as Katherine Pleydell-Bouverie.

The United States enjoyed a heady triumph at the 1900 Exposition Universelle in Paris, which made world leaders of such potteries as Rookwood Pottery (Cincinnati), Newcomb Pottery (New Orleans), Grueby Faience Company (Boston), Pewabic Pottery (Detroit), Van Briggle Pottery (Colorado Springs), Moravian Pottery and Tile Works (Doylestown, Pennsylvania), and Clifton Art Pottery (Newark). Earthenware vessels with nature themes were finished in satiny matte finishes in plant colors, especially greens and blues.

Important educators in the field included Taxile Doat, a Frenchman who was associated with University City Pottery in Missouri, and Charles Fergus Binns of the New York College of Clayworking and Ceramics.

In Great Britain, William De Morgan's preference for Spanish, Moorish, and Italian ceramics, decorated with glowing enameled plant and bird forms, influenced artisans at the Ruskin Pottery (West Smethwick), Della Robbia Pottery (Berkinhead), and St. Ives Pottery (Cornwall) as well as his own workshop (Surrey and, later, London).

Some of the most exotic work came from "the mad potter of Biloxi," George Ohr of the Biloxi (Mississippi) Art Pottery. Fascinating to see, it was in many cases impossible to use.

It may be imagined with what abandon the women of that time, whose efforts had been directed to the making of antimacassars or woolen Afghans, threw themselves into the fascinating occupation of working in wet clay. . . .

—Mary Louise McLaughlin, *Bulletin of the American Ceramic Society,* May 1938

Robert R. Jarvie's silver pitcher—presented as a wedding gift in 1911— recalls the linear forms of Charles Rennie Mackintosh's work.

Hardware often bore distinct chisel marks to link it to the artisan. Copper was popular and sometimes came with a bright-and-dull "antique" finish.

From recently established firms such as Tiffany and Gorham came new, seductively simple designs for old standbys, notably teapots, coffeepots, and pitchers. Much fine silver was produced in England and the United States, in designs reminiscent of medieval work. The look was intentionally handmade.

Precious metals, however, were not the stars of the period, which might be called the copper age, particularly in America. The humble metal served for everything from decorative door hinges, furniture hardware, and fireplace hoods to lamps, vases, and jewelry. Roycroft was especially noted for its fine copper work. Silver and copper were also used in combination, with silver inlays picking out designs on patinated copper surfaces.

Limitations were turned into virtues. Hand-formed and beaten objects clearly showed the imprint of the tools that shaped them, distinguishing the result from machine work. Much fine, handmade jewelry used inlaid silver and semiprecious stones such as opals or even glass rather than gold and gems. Pewter and Tudric ware from England's Liberty and Company reached a wide public on both continents, and bronze and iron were used as well.

The machine age generated not just housing for a burgeoning middle class and millions of factory workers but also the factories themselves. Industrial society needed schools and universities, apartment buildings, government offices, warehouses, stores, restaurants, and railroad terminals. Still, Arts and Crafts architects generally remained at odds with the machine-built environment, focusing instead on human-scale structures: houses and churches.

The simple lines of the Grove Park Inn (1913, Fred L. Seely), Asheville, North Carolina, are made monumental by large, smooth stones used for the walls.

Grove Park Inn
Asheville N.C.   Robinson

In his magazine (above), Stickley urged home-owners to be true craftsmen and build their own houses. His workshop filled orders for plans for Craftsman houses such as this 1904 bungalow (opposite). Stickley, of course, showed how to complete these comfortable homes—with Craftsman furnishings.

In the United States the most important popular expression of the Arts and Crafts movement was the Craftsman house—usually a bungalow or a Four Square. Under the influence of magazines such as *The Craftsman* and *The Bungalow,* as well as catalogues of ready-cut houses (from Sears, Roebuck, Montgomery Ward, and Aladdin, among others) and ready-to-use plans, both building types flourished between 1905 and 1920.

Adapted from the small dwellings of nineteenth-century British colonial officials in India, the bungalow's low, horizontal lines, broad, gabled roofs, and generous porches appealed to thousands, spreading quickly from California to every corner of the nation. The boxy Four Square, with its compact, four-room plan, became a ubiquitous feature of small towns and suburbs. Executed in cement blocks, poured concrete, stucco, structural tile, brick, shingle, or weatherboard, both house types were generally undecorated, claiming interest through sheltering eaves with exposed rafter ends, distinctive dormers, and imaginative porches.

Bowen Court (1912, Alfred Heineman), Pasadena, California, was one of many bungalow courts that sprang up in the West (pages 74–75).

The 1907 Blacker House in Pasadena, designed by Charles Sumner Greene (opposite, top) and Henry Mather Greene (below), was the grandest of their "ultimate bungalows."

Spacious single-family houses exemplified the Arts and Crafts ideal of home. Based on—but never directly copied from—regional, vernacular building types, the architect-designed Arts and Crafts house took many forms.

It began with Philip Webb's 1859 design for William Morris's Red House in Kent. In the hands of English architects such as Webb, C. F. A. Voysey, and W. R. Lethaby, these houses might resemble an old Cotswold cottage. Or, they could, like the house at 25 Cadogan Gardens in London (1899, Arthur Heygate Mackmurdo), suggest an Old English city house. Charles Rennie Mackintosh carried the movement to Scotland.

In the eastern United States, Wilson Eyre, Frank Miles Day, and others provided wealthy clients with an interpretation of the colonial farmhouse of British or Dutch settlers. In the Midwest, Frank Lloyd Wright and his colleagues produced Prairie School houses, perhaps best exemplified by Wright's Robie House (1908) in Chicago. In the West, Greene and Greene's Gamble House (1909) in Pasadena, California—a luxurious bungalow—is one of the most famous of the architect-designed Arts and Crafts houses. For a select group of clients the Greene brothers produced powerful expressions in wood that were married to their landscapes and suited to the hot California climate.

GARDEN CITIES

In English greenbelt towns, forests and farmland swathed the cities. Letchworth (1904, Parker and Unwin) included a municipal center, a discreetly placed factory district, and a broad edging of agricultural land. Its amenities were accessible to all residents.

Town and country must be married, *and out of this joyous union will spring a new hope, a new life, a new civilization.*
—Ebenezer Howard, *Garden Cities of Tomorrow*, 1898

Horrified by the deplorable living conditions of most English industrial workers, social reformers called for healthful, well-planned working-class communities—"garden cities"—such as Bournville (1898) and Port Sunlight (1899) near Birmingham.

Industrial sponsors established model company towns with houses designed by such notable Arts and Crafts architects as Parker and Unwin. Heightened social consciousness in the United States led to tenement reform, industry-supported housing, and, later, government-sponsored garden communities like Hilton Village (1919) in Newport News, Virginia.

Complementing garden cities was the City Beautiful movement that blossomed after the 1893 World's Columbian Exposition. Waterfronts were reclaimed, urban parks organized, and broad, tree-lined avenues and curving parkways laid out, as America set out to rival European centers. Frederick Law Olmsted, Sr. and Jr., John Nolen, and architects such as Daniel Burnham conceived brilliant plans for civic improvement, replete with grand buildings. In Vienna broad avenues replaced the ancient city walls, while Paris was paved with new boulevards by Baron Haussmann.

CHURCHES

Arts and Crafts architects tended to have a far more secular outlook than their Gothic Revival predecessors, but their interest in church architecture remained strong.

In the United States a renewed interest in the early Spanish missions of California, Arizona, and New Mexico led to their study and, in many cases, restoration. It also spurred an interpretive revival of Mission architecture that was not confined to the American Southwest—nor even to the design of churches.

In a different vein is Bernard Maybeck's First Church of Christ, Scientist (1911) in Berkeley, California. The major Arts and Crafts church building in the United States, it is a California blend of wood, natural finishes, pergolas, and porches, with inserted Gothic decoration. A sparser, more Craftsman-like example, also in Berkeley, is St. John's Presbyterian Church (1910, Julia Morgan).

Like many Arts and Crafts churches in England, London's Holy Trinity, Sloane Street (1900, John Dando Sedding), is a splendid Arts and Crafts interpretation of the Gothic style with distinctive ornament. Watts Chapel (1898, Mary Watts), Compton, Surrey, also has important period interior decoration.

Almost mystical in its extensive use of bold Gothic ornament in an Arts and Crafts frame, the First Church of Christ, Scientist, is Maybeck's masterwork.

Once a student at the Ecole des Beaux-Arts, Maybeck was at home in a variety of idioms, from classical to Arts and Crafts.

The development of rein-
forced concrete in the mid-
nineteenth century promised
buildings that were almost
fireproof, while the elevator
meant that they could rise
higher than a person's legs
could gladly climb. But the

Arts and Crafts movement, dedicated to
handcraftsmanship and natural materials,
was largely unimpressed by big buildings.

Arts and Crafts architects, nonetheless,
were not averse to applying the movement's
principles to some modern building types.
The Black Friar Pub (1905, H. Fuller Clark),
London, is a picturesque Old English public
house in a dense urban setting. The Amsterdam Shipping Offices (1916, J. M. Van der
Mey) in the Netherlands is one of the few notable Arts and Crafts office buildings. London's Boulting and Sons office block (1903, H.
Fuller Clark) was designed in the picturesque
English mode, with colorful mosaic panels.

In Chicago, Louis Sullivan's distinctive or-
nament embellished the Carson, Pirie, Scott
Department Store (1903), while Frank Lloyd
Wright remodeled the court of the Rookery
Building (1905) in Sullivanesque style.

London's Black Friar
Pub (opposite and
above) was an Arts and
Crafts idealization of
the traditional English
pub. It managed to be
evocative, creative—
and irresistibly playful.

Best Addresses

Magpie and Stump
(1894, C. R. Ashbee),
London
Pewabic Pottery (1906,
William B. Stratton),
Detroit
Merchants Bank (1912,
Purcell, Feick and
Elmslie), Winona,
Minnesota

With larger cities and more affluent citizens came the demand for more schools, universities, and museums. Arts and Crafts designers made distinguished, if not numerous, contributions to this new building need.

Among the most important Arts and Crafts manifestations of this phenomenon is Charles Rennie Mackintosh's Glasgow School of Art (1909) in Scotland. Finland's National Museum, the Kansallismuseo (1912, Gesellius, Lindgren, and Saarinen), Helsinki, dramatically illustrates the quest for national identity through the use of regional traditions wrapped in the new cloth of the Arts and Crafts.

In Philadelphia the University of Pennsylvania Museum (1893–1926, Wilson Eyre, Frank Miles Day and Brother, and Cope and Stewardson) is a masterpiece of the picturesque English Arts and Crafts. Joseph Maria Olbrich's Austellungshaus der Wiener Sezession (1898), a small exhibition building in Vienna, breaks headlong from classical traditions to embrace the new designs of the Secessionist movement. London's Horniman Museum (1901, Charles H. Townsend) demonstrates a creative, eclectic espousal of picturesque Arts and Crafts ideals.

With its arcades and plain white stucco walls, the La Jolla Women's Club (1914, Irving Gill), La Jolla, California, adapted the Mission traditions of California to the Arts and Crafts grammar of simplicity.

There is something very restful and satisfying to my mind in the simple cube house with creamy walls, sheer and plain. . . .
—Irving Gill, "The Home of the Future," *The Craftsman*, May 1916

ENTERTAINMENT

Chautauqua performances carried fun and education to small towns in the United States. The 1870s amphitheater in Chautauqua, New York, was designed by movement founder Lewis Miller. Trunklike columns and branched roof supports symbolized the first venue for Chautauqua presentations: in the open air, sheltered only by trees.

Hits of the Day

H.M.S. Pinafore (1878, Gilbert and Sullivan)

Hedda Gabler (1890, Henrik Ibsen)

The Merry Widow (1905, Franz Lehár)

Sweethearts (1913, Victor Herbert)

Maytime (1917, Sigmund Romberg)

Large theaters and sports arenas were not the kinds of structures that Arts and Crafts architects were most likely to design. However, restaurants such as Miss Catherine Cranston's four celebrated Glasgow tearooms (1901–11), designed by Charles Rennie Mackintosh and decorated by him and his wife, Margaret Macdonald, provided opportunities for convivial eating, imbibing, and socializing in an appropriately artistic setting.

A stimulating blend of art, social purpose, and high spirits typified Arts and Crafts entertainment. George Bernard Shaw noted that William Morris's comedy *The Tables Turned, or Nupkins Awakened*, written in 1887 as a socialist fund-raiser, left his audience "rolling, wallowing, [and] guffawing." Vaudeville and music halls brought more lighthearted antics, and a string of Gilbert and Sullivan operettas such as *The Mikado* (1885) entertained audiences on both sides of the Atlantic.

Long walks on country roads and through urban parkland were among the activities preferred by seekers after the simple life. As a healthful escape from city stress, they also took enthusiastically to camping out, often in simple log structures that exemplified the Arts and Crafts aesthetic.

Inside the Old Faithful Inn (1903, Robert C. Reamer) at Yellowstone National Park, Wyoming, treelike balconies surround a six-story atrium. A massive stone chimney provides a welcoming hearth, the center of the Arts and Crafts philosophy.

Grand Hotels

American Hotel
  and Cafe (1901,
  Willem Kromhout),
  Amsterdam
Mohonk Mountain
  House (1879–1910),
  Lake Mohonk,
  New York
Mission Inn (1903,
  Arthur Benton),
  Riverside, California
Awahnee Inn (1927,
  Gilbert S. Under-
  wood), Yosemite
  Park, California

Trains seemed to go everywhere in the late nineteenth century. Large "union" terminals, mostly classical in style, eliminated the tangle of uncoordinated tracks that had mocked the Arts and Crafts ideal of clean and orderly cities. Small-town stations were sometimes designed in the Arts and Crafts idiom, with deep, plain-bracketed eaves and swooping rooflines. This became the era of the great railroad hotel, as rail and auto travelers discovered the American West and its wealth of Indian and Spanish colonial images.

One place people went was simply out of town—to placid lakes and forests that spelled escape from modern life. Vacation cottages and rambling resorts offered rustic havens suited to the Arts and Crafts lifestyle. Rugged cabins sprang up from the mountains in the East to national parks in the West. Sunny states like California and Florida made room for new residents and visitors alike in thrifty bungalows and bungalow courts. Retreats for the wealthy—euphemistically called "camps" in the Adirondacks—synthesized Arts and Crafts precepts down to adze marks left in the logs. Gustav Stickley himself built a Craftsman log house in New Jersey, just an easy rail commute from his office in New York City.

SOURCES OF INFORMATION

American Bungalow Magazine
P.O. Box 756
Sierra Madre, Calif.
91025-0756

Craftsman Home Owners
Roycroft Associates
31 South Grove Street
East Aurora, N.Y. 14052

Cooper-Hewitt Museum
2 East 91st Street
New York, N.Y. 10128

Decorative Arts Society
c/o Brooklyn Museum
200 Eastern Parkway
Brooklyn, N.Y. 11238

Gamble House Bookstore
4 Westmoreland Place
Pasadena, Calif. 91103

Greene and Greene Center for the Study of the Arts and Crafts Movement in America
Huntington Library
1151 Oxford Road
San Marino, Calif. 91108

Moravian Pottery and Tile Works
Bucks County
Department of Parks and Recreation
Swamp Road
Doylestown, Pa. 18901

National Trust for Historic Preservation
1785 Massachusetts Avenue, N.W.
Washington, D.C. 20036

National Trust for Places of Historic Interest or Natural Beauty
36 Queen Anne's Gate
London SW1H 9AS,
England

Society of Architectural Historians
1232 Pine Street
Philadelphia, Pa.
19107-5944

Tile Heritage Foundation
Box 1850
Healdsburg, Calif. 95448

Victorian Society
1 Priory Gardens
Bedford Park
London W4 1TT,
England

Victorian Society in America
219 South Sixth Street
Philadelphia, Pa. 19106

William Morris Society
Kelmscott House
26 Upper Mall
Hammersmith
London W6 9TA,
England

ADDITIONAL SITES TO VISIT

*See also places cited
in the text.*

Adirondack Museum
Blue Mountain Lake, N.Y.

Craftsman Farms (1910)
Morris Plains, N.J.

**Frank Lloyd Wright
Home and Studio**
(1889–1909)
Oak Park, Ill.

Forest Hills Gardens
(1909)
Queens, N.Y.

**Frederick Law Olmsted
National Historic Site**
(1880s–)
Brookline, Mass.

Gamble House (1909)
Pasadena, Calif.

Grove Park Inn (1913)
Asheville, N.C.

Guild of Handicraft
Chipping Campden,
Gloucestershire, England

Hill House (1904)
Helensburgh, Scotland

Horniman Museum
(1901)
London, England

Little Thakeham (1902)
Storrington, England

Munstead Wood Garden
(1896)
Surrey, England

The Orchard (1899)
Chorley Wood
Hertfordshire, England

Rodmarton Manor
(1929)
Gloucestershire, England

Roycroft Community
(1893)
East Aurora, N.Y.

Shaw's Corner (1906)
Ayot St. Lawrence
Hertfordshire, England

Standen (1894)
East Grinstead
West Sussex, England

**University of
Pennsylvania Museum**
(1893–1926)
Philadelphia, Pa.

**Victoria and Albert
Museum**
William Morris Room
London, England

Wightwick Manor (1893)
Wolverhampton, England

William Morris Gallery
London, England

RECOMMENDED READING

Clark, Garth, and
Margie Hughto.
*A Century of Ceramics
in the United States,
1878–1978*. New
York: E. P. Dutton,
1979.

Clark, Robert Hudson,
ed. *The Arts and
Crafts Movement in
America 1876–1976*.
Princeton, N.J.: Prince-
ton University Press,
1972.

Cumming, Elizabeth,
and Wendy Kaplan.
*The Arts and Crafts
Movement*. New York:
Thames and Hudson,
1991.

Davey, Peter. *Architec-
ture of the Arts and
Crafts Movement*.
New York: Rizzoli,
1980.

Kaplan, Wendy. *The Art
That Is Life: The Arts
and Crafts Movement
in America, 1875–
1920*. Boston: Little,
Brown, 1987.

Kardon, Janet, ed. *The
Ideal Home, 1900–
1920: The History of
Twentieth-Century
American Craft*. New
York: Abrams and the
American Craft
Museum, 1993.

Lancaster, Clay. *The
American Bungalow*.
New York: Abbeville
Press, 1985.

Makinson, Randell L.
*Greene and Greene:
Architecture as Fine
Art*. Salt Lake City:
Peregrine Smith, 1977.
———. *Greene and
Greene: Furniture and
Related Designs*. Salt
Lake City: Peregrine
Smith, 1979.

Mayer, Barbara. *In the
Arts and Crafts Style*.
San Francisco: Chroni-
cle Books, 1992.

Naylor, Gillian. *The Arts
and Crafts Movement*.
Cambridge: MIT Press,
1971.

Smith, Mary Ann.
*Gustav Stickley, The
Craftsman*. Syracuse,
N.Y.: Syracuse Univer-
sity Press, 1983.

Trapp, Kenneth R., et al.
*The Arts and Crafts
Movement in Califor-
nia: Living the Good
Life*. New York: Abbe-
ville Press; Oakland:
Oakland Museum,
1993.

Volpe, Tod M., and Beth
Cathers. *Treasures
of the American Arts
and Crafts Movement,
1890–1920*. London:
Thames and Hudson,
1988.

INDEX

Page numbers in italics refer to illustrations.

Aladdin homes, 72
Amsterdam Shipping Offices, 83
Animal Locomotion, 10
architectural features, 20–21, 22–23, 30–31
Armstrong, Margaret, 65
Art Nouveau, 24, 61
Arts and Crafts Exhibition Society, 7
Ashbee, C. R., 24, 26, 83
Associated Artists, 45
Austellungshaus der Wiener Sezession, 26, 85

The Barn, *30*
Barnsley, Sidney, 27
Barnsley, Ernest, 27
Batchelder, Ernest Allen, 27
Beardsley, Aubrey, 27, 65
Biloxi Art Pottery, 67
Binns, Charles Fergus, 67
Blacker House, 26, 51, *76–77*
Black Friar Pub, *82, 83*
Bok, Edward William, 26
Boulting and Sons, 83
Bournville, 27, 78
Bowen Court, *74–75*, 76
Bradley, Will, 27, 65
Bradley, His Book, 64
building materials, 22, 28, 32–33, 34
building types, 70–89
built-in furniture, *48–49*, *52–53*, 54–55
The Bungalow, 72
bungalows, 21, 22, 31, 32, 55, 72, *73, 74–75*, 88
Burden, Jane, 62
Burne-Jones, Edward, 62
Burnham, Daniel, 78

carpets, 45
Carson, Pirie, Scott Department Store, 83
Cassatt, Mary, 62
Chautauqua, N.Y., *87*
churches, 80–81
city planners, 27, 37, 78
Clark, H. Fuller, 83

Clifton Art Pottery, 66, 67
colors and paint, 22, 32, 42–43
commercial buildings, 82–83
Cope and Stewardson, 85
The Craftsman, 21, 24, 26, 51, 72, 85
Craftsman Farms, *4-5*, 26, 96
Craftsman Homes, 21, 26
Craftsman style, 21, 22, 31, 40, 55, 72
Cragside, *14*
Crane, Walter, 27, 43, 62
Crystal Palace, 6
curtains, 58

Day, Frank Miles, 77, 85
Della Robbia Pottery, 67
De Morgan, William, 27, 67
Doat, Taxile, 67
doors, 22, 31
Dow, Arthur Wesley, 27
Dresser, Christopher, 43
Durant, William, 28

Edison, Thomas, 10, 11, 32
Ellis, Harvey, 27
entertainment, 86–87
Everard Printing Works, *35*
Eyre, Wilson, 24, 26, 77, 85

fashion, clothing, 16
fine arts, 62–63
fireplaces, *14*, 40–41
First Church of Christ, Scientist, 26, *80*, 81
floors, 44–45
furnishings, 48–69
furniture, 50–55

Gamble House, *2*, 26, *38–39*, 58, 77, 96
garden cities, 24, 78–79
gardens, 24, 36–37
Gesellius, Lindgren, and Saarinen, 85
Gilbert and Sullivan, 86
Gilchrist, Edmund, 26
Gill, Irving, 26, 31, 85
Glasgow School of Art, 26, 85
Goddards, 26, 27
Gorham silver, 68
Gothic Revival style, 6–7, 18

graphic arts, 64–65
Greenaway, Kate, 43
Green Dining Room, *42*
Greene, Charles Sumner, 24, 26, 38, *77*
Greene, Henry Mather, 24, 26, *77*
Greene and Greene, 21, 22, 31, 34, 49, 51, 55, 58, 77, 96
Green Gables, *20*
Griffin, Marion Mahony, 9, 26
Griffin, Walter Burley, 9, 26
Grove Park Inn, *70–71*
Grueby, William Henry, 27
Grueby Faience Company, 27, 66

Hall, E. T. and E. S., 32
Hampstead Garden Suburb, 26
hardware, 34, 68
Haslemere Peasant Industries, 56
Haussmann, Baron Georges-Eugène, 78
Hawley House, *41*
Heineman, Alfred, 76
Hill House, *25*, 26
Hilton Village, 78
Hoffmann, Josef, 24
Holy Trinity, Sloane Street, 81
Horniman Museum, 85
House and Garden, 37
houses, 21, 72–77, 88
Howard, Ebenezer, 27, 78
Hubbard, Elbert, 24, 26, 65
Hunter, Dard, 27, 61

illustrators, 27, 43, 62, 65
industrial revolution, 6, 10, 70
Ingersoll Terrace, 32
Irwin House, *23*

Jarvie, Robert R., 68
Jekyll, Gertrude, 24, 27, 37
Jensen, Georg, 27
Jensen, Jens, 27, 37

Kansallismuseo (Finland's National Museum), 26, 85
Kelmscott Press, 26, 65
Keramic Studio, 27, 66

Ladies' Home Journal, 26
La Farge, John, 27, 34, 58

La Jolla Women's Club, 26, *84*
landscape architects, 24, 27, 37, 78
Letchworth, *79*
Lethaby, W. R., 24, 26, 76
Liberty, Arthur Lasenby, 32
Liberty and Company, *33*, 68
lighting, *1*, 60–61
Limbert, Charles P., 27, 50
Low, John Gardner, 27
Lutyens, Edwin, 24, 26, 37

Macdonald, Frances, 27
Macdonald, Margaret, 27, 86
Mackintosh, Charles Rennie, 24, 26, 51, 68, 76, 85, 86
Mackmurdo, Arthur Heygate, 26, 76
Maybeck, Bernard, 24, 26, 31, *81*
McLaughlin, Mary Louise, 66, 67
mechanical systems, 46–47
Mercer, Henry Chapman, 26, 45
metalwork, 34, 68–69
middle class, growth of, 14–15
Miller, Lewis, 86
Mission style, 40, 50, 55, 81, 85
Montgomery Ward, 72
Moravian Pottery and Tile Works, 26, 45, 66
Morgan, Julia, 26, 81
Morris, May, 27, *56*
Morris, William, 6, 7, 18, 21, 22, 24, 26, 34, 43, 45, *56*, 62, 65, 76, 86, 96
Morris and Company, 15, 26, 45
Mott Iron Works, *46*, *47*
movement leaders, 24, 26
Munstead Wood, 27, *36*
museums, 85
Muybridge, Eadweard, 10

Neatby, W. J., 34
Newcomb Pottery, 66
New York College of Clayworking and Ceramics, 67
Nichols, Maria Longworth, 16, 27, 66
Niedecken, George, 27, 51
Nolen, John, 27

Ohr, George, 67
Olbrich, Joseph Maria, 24, 26, 85

Old Faithful Inn, *89*
Olmsted, Frederick Law, 37, 78
Olmsted, Frederick Law, Jr., 27, 37, 78
The Orchard, 26
ornament, 22, 34–35

Parker, Barry, 26
Parker and Unwin, 78
parks, 37, 78
Pewabic Pottery, 66, 83
plans, 22
Pleydell-Bouverie, Katherine, 66
porches, 22, 31, 37
Port Sunlight, 78
pottery, *17*, 66–67
Prairie School, 21, 22, 32, 55, 77
Pre-Raphaelites, 62
Price, Bruce, 26
Price, William, 26
Prior, Edward Schroder, 31, 32
Progressive Era, 9, 11
Purcell, Feick and Elmslie, 83
Pyle, Howard, 62

Reamer, Robert C., 88
Red House, *18–19, 23*, 26, 76
Reeve House, *48–49*
reform movement, 6, 11, 16, 78
Rhead, Louis, 65
Robie House, *52–53*, 55, 77
Robineau, Adelaide Alsop, 27, 66
Rock Crest–Rock Glen, *8–9*, 26
Rohlfs, Charles, 27
roofs, 22, 31, 34
Rookery Building, 83
Rookwood Pottery, 16, 27, 66
Rose Valley Community, 26
Rossetti, Dante Gabriel, 62
Roycroft Community, 24, 26, 27, 68
Roycroft Inn, 40, *60*
Roycroft Press, 65
Ruskin, John, 6, 7, 16, 26, 62
Ruskin Pottery, 67

Saarinen, Eliel, 26, 85
Sagamore, *28–29*
The Salutation of Beatrice, *63*
Schmidt, Charles, 66
schools, 85
Scott, M. H. Baillie, 24, 26

Sears, Roebuck, 55, 72
Sedding, John Dando, 81
Seely, Fred L., 70
Shaw, George Bernard, 86
Shaw, Richard Norman, 15
Shay, Felix, 61
stained glass, 34, 58, 59
Stickley, Gustav, 7, *21*, 24, 26, 50, 51, 72, 88, 96
St. Ives Pottery, 67
St. John's Presbyterian Church, 26, 81
Sullivan, Louis, 83

textiles, 45, 56–57, 58
Tiffany, Louis, 27, 34, 45, 58, 61
Tiffany Studios, 27, 58, 68
timeline, 12–13
Toulouse-Lautrec, Henri de, 65
Townsend, Charles H., 85
transportation, 15, 88
25 Cadogan Gardens, 26, 76

University City Pottery, 67
University of Pennsylvania Museum, 26, 85
Unwin, Raymond, 26

Van Briggle Pottery, 66
Vanderbilt, Alfred, *29*
Van der Mey, J. M., 83
Van Erp, Dirk, 27, 61, 96
Victoria (queen of England), 10
Victoria and Albert Museum, *43*
Voysey, C. F. A., 24, 26, 76

wallpapers, 42–43, 96
walls, 40–43
Watts, Mary, 81
Watts Chapel, 81
Webb, Philip, 18, 26, 76
Wheeler, Candace, 27, 45, 56
Whistler, James MacNeill, 62
windows, 22, 31, 58–59
The Works of Geoffrey Chaucer, 65
Wright, Frank Lloyd, 24, 26, 31, 32, 34, 45, 50, 51, 55, 58, 77, 83
Wyeth, N. C., 65

Yellin, Samuel, 27

CREDITS

Adirondack Museum: 28–29

American Museum of Natural History, Department of Library Services: 10–11 (negative number 336792)

© Wayne Andrews, Esto: 80

Arthur Sanderson and Sons Ltd: endpapers

Art Institute of Chicago, photographs © 1994. All rights reserved: 8–9 (Walter Burley Griffin and Marion Mahony Griffin, American, partnership 1911–1937. Detail of perspective rendering of Rock Crest/Rock Glen, Mason City, Iowa, lithograph and gouache on green satin, c. 1912, 59 × 201 cm. Gift of Marion Mahony Griffin through Eric Nicholls, 1988.182); 69 (Robert Riddle Jarvie, Chicago, Illinois, 1865–1941. Pitcher, silver, 1911, 10¼ × 8 in., base diam.: 6⁷⁄₁₆ in. Gift of Raymond W. Sheets, 1973.357)

Brass Light Gallery, Inc.: 61

Bucks County Historical Society: 45

Buffalo Studios, California: 68

Catalogue "G" Illustrating the Plumbing and Sanitary Department (J. L. Mott Iron Works, 1888): 46, 47

Cathers and Dembrosky: 1, 51

Centre Canadien d'Architecture/ Canadian Centre for Architecture, Montréal: 52–53

Martin Charles: 18–19

Charles Hosmer Morse Museum of American Art, Winter Park, Fla.: 59

Chautauqua Institution Archives: 87

Cincinnati Historical Society: 17 (B-87–302)

College of Environmental Design Documents Collection, University of California at Berkeley: 48–49, 81

Country Life Picture Library: 14, 36

Craftsman Farms Foundation, Parsippany, N.J.: 4–5

Craftsman Homes (Stickley, 2d ed., 1909): 21, 73

First Garden City Heritage Museum, Letchworth Garden City: 79

Greene and Greene Library, Gamble House, University of Southern California: 74–75, 76–77, 77 (top and bottom)

Grove Park Inn Resort: 70–71

Historic American Buildings Survey: 20, 23 (bottom), 84

David W. Lowden: 72

Maryland Historical Society, Baltimore: 41

Montana Historical Society: 89

Museum of Fine Arts, Boston: 60 (Harriet Otis Cruft Fund); 64 (Lee M. Friedman Fund)

Music: A Pictorial Archive of Woodcuts and Engravings (Dover, 1980): 11

National Monuments Record, © RCHME Crown Copyright: 23 (top), 30, 31, 33, 35, 82, 83

National Portrait Gallery, London: 56

Newark Museum: 66 (purchase 1914); 67 (gift of Mrs.Constance B. Benson, 1977)

Old-House Journal: 54 (September–October 1994, Gloucester, Mass. 01930)

Marvin Rand: 2, 50

Reed International Books Ltd.: 44

© Royal Commission on the Ancient and Historical Monuments of Scotland: 25

Scalamandré: 57

Tim Street-Porter: 38–39

Toledo Museum of Art: 63 (purchased with funds from the Libbey Endowment, gift of Edward Drummond Libbey)

Victoria and Albert Museum Picture Library: 42

The Works of Geoffrey Chaucer (Morris, 1896): 65

Produced by Archetype Press, Inc.
Project Director: Diane Maddex
Editor: Gretchen Smith Mui
Editorial Assistant: Kristi Flis
Art Director: Robert L. Wiser

Other titles in the Abbeville StyleBooks™ series include *Art Deco* (ISBN 1-55859-824-3); *Early Victorian* (ISBN 0-7892-0011-2); and *Gothic Revival* (ISBN 1-55859-823-5).

Library of Congress Cataloging-in-Publication Data
Massey, James C.
Arts & crafts / James Massey & Shirley Maxwell.
    p.   cm. — (Stylebooks)
Includes bibliographical references (p. 92) and index.
ISBN 0-7892-0010-4
1. Arts and crafts movement. I. Maxwell, Shirley.
II. Title. III. Title: Arts and crafts. IV. Series.
NK1140.M38 1995
745'.4'441–dc20   94-43397